# Ultimate Cures To Curb Anxiety

### Get free from Anxiety, get your life back

## AMARPREET SINGH

Publisher - The Thought Flame

THE THOUGHT FLAME
TURNING SPARK INTO FLAME

info@thethoughtflame.com

www.thethoughtflame.com

# Table of Contents

# Introduction

We all have panicked or worried about difficult situations in our lives. Sometimes over yet to be finished assignment, sometimes over a troublesome financial period or sometimes when a family member has fallen ill severely. This is normal and necessary to avert serious dangers.

However, have you ever had sweaty cold palms without any reason? Do you over think about simple conversations or situations? Do you have problems concentrating because your mind is pre-occupied with other worries? Does this sound familiar- heart beating fast, there is shallow breathing and unimaginable thoughts and feelings over whelming you? Or do you feel like anxiety is dictating every move of yours?

While it is completely normal to feel anxious for a short period of time, there can be chances where your anxiety does not subside at all. Anxiety that is continual , that is without any prominent reason and cause can wreak havoc on your daily life. This condition is termed as Anxiety disorder.

In this book you will find every detail about the signs, symptoms and types of anxiety disorder. It will also inform you about the telltale signs of anxiety disorder among kids. You will learn about natural alternative ways to treat anxiety without having to resort to harmful prescription medications.

There is no need to continue living with anxiety. You can put an end to it. Self-awareness is the key. You will equip yourselves with homemade remedies that are safe, easy to get from your kitchen shelves or garden and simple to make.

So, what are you waiting for? Let's beat this anxiety together so you can begin living the stress free life that you deserve

# Chapter One: Anxiety and Its Effects on The Human Body

Do you sometimes feel your stomach churning, hands sweating profusely and yet without a reason? Does it affect both your physical and mental behavior? Sometimes , anxiety is normal and can be controlled. However at times it can go out of control and hamper your daily lives prominently.

There can be situations when you just cannot act like before you used to because now anxiety has taken a grip of you. It is the feeling of being afraid of the unknown. On a broader sense, anxiety comes in different forms – sometimes feeling worried, apprehensive, being nervous or plainly everything going out of control. Severe forms of anxiety can be extremely devastating and can have a great impact on your life and health.

# Understanding The Condition of Anxiety

Fear and panic are natural human emotions. Everyone has felt anxious for one reason or another. It is the feeling of worry, apprehension or panic in response to certain situations which is usually unsafe or uncomfortable.

You may have experienced anxiety during a job interview. Or perhaps you've experienced a heightened sense of alertness when you felt that you were in danger. In a sense, anxiety and panic is your body's way of informing you that it feels threatened. To a certain extent , it is important because it helps you stay safe.

Anxiety can be useful when it helps you deal with dangerous situations. It can actually push you to study for an exam, or it can convince you to leave a dangerous situation .

However, like many things, it can be detrimental when taken to the extreme. It can be counterproductive and it might prevent you from achieving your full potential.

Anxiety is a basic human emotion . Generally speaking, it is healthy and manageable to a certain degree. Because everyone experiences anxiety, it can be challenging to recognize and accept anxiety as a  problem, however if you just ignore the symptoms of anxiety, you miss the chance to understand your life and yourself better. If you try to understand what your anxiety is telling you, you will have a better chance of overcoming the problem. In effect, you get to enjoy a better quality of life.

Is your anxiety helping you or has it become excessive and detrimental? We'll now try to learn more about anxiety and what you can do to help control the problem.

## How Much Anxiety Is Too Much?

Some level of anxiety is normal. It is what pushes you to watch over your children. It makes you fasten your seat belts when riding a car. It keeps people safe in general . This level of worry shouldn't really interfere with your daily life. On the contrary, it is necessary for our own protection.

In general, anxiety is based on the "flight-or-fight" response brought about by a stressful event. It can be seen as a response to an actual situation of threat or danger. When a normal anxiety response is taken to another level, then it can be considered as an anxiety disorder.

Once this happens, anxiety starts to control your life, instead of contributing to it positively.

Typically, the "flight-or-fight" response should be attached to a stressful situation. However, when a person is worried or anxious for no specific reason, then it can be problematic. An anxiety disorder can disrupt the daily flow of life. It can be very problematic because it cannot be controlled nor understood thoroughly by the sufferer. If it is persistent and excessive, it can be disabling. You might find yourself unable to go through your daily routine in a smooth manner.

While I know that it can be difficult to assess your own anxiety, and it is always best to see an expert that can make a diagnosis. However, regardless of how mild or severe your condition might be, it pays to understand more about your own situation.

# What Is A True Panic Attack?

A panic attack can be frightening. It is a combination of physical and psychological symptoms that could leave a person scared and worried for no clear reason. It is an exaggerated response to fear and anxiety or even something positive like excitement. Physically, there is a build-up of an uncomfortable sensation.

The symptoms of anxiety vary per person, but generally speaking , one who is experiencing an anxiety disorder might end up with chest pains, breathing difficulties, sweating and nausea. On a psychological level, there is an irrational amount of fear. Some are convinced that they are going mad, and others are convinced that they are going to die. It can be a truly terrifying experience.

Panic attacks usually last for about five to ten minutes although there have been reports of panic attacks lasting for up to one hour. There are also different levels of anxiety attacks. Some might be intense and life-changing, while others could be milder and much easier to handle.

It's hard to point out a trigger of a panic attack. Most attacks start and stop at random. There is really no single trigger . Some attacks can even happen in the middle of the night. It could wake you up for no particular reason. Night - time attacks can be particularly frightening, especially if you sleep alone. Panic attacks may occur only once in a lifetime or they may occur as often as several times a week. Some cases of panic attacks are even genetic.

# Are People More Susceptible To Having More Panic Attacks Than Others?

You can be having a lot of panic attacks for a variety of reasons. It can be because of your personality, your childhood experiences, your genetic makeup or your current life situation. In most cases, it is a mixture of various things which makes a person susceptible to anxiety attacks.

Your past experiences can greatly influence your anxieties in the present. What were your fears in the past? If you faced certain fears or worries that you weren't able to overcome, you might experience the same level of anxiety when facing a similar situation. Whatever you experienced in childhood could strongly influence your adult life. If you had a traumatic experience as a child, it is very likely that you will feel a lot of anxiety as an adult. Look back and try to recall if you experienced anything major that might make you feel anxious or panicky.

People who don't feel a sense of security in their current life situation are also likely to feel anxious as well. For example, although you may have a job, you might still feel anxious if you feel that it is not a secure job.

The important thing to remember about anxiety is that it is essentially just a fear of what can happen in the future. It is about not finding peace in your current life situation and worrying about things that may or may not happen in future.

# Five Common Myths About Anxiety

It is often noticed that most people do not recognize their anxiety instead they understand it as something is wrong with them. Some people try suppressing common symptoms of anxiety with temporary medicines. While a few view it as weird or something unusual. Therefore , the first step in anxiety management is to differentiate between myth and facts.

## Myth #1: Anxiety Is Something That Lasts Forever

A person, who feels anxious often, might assume it as a permanent state of mind and body. Anxiety in fact temporary can be done away with medications, lifestyle changes and exercises.

13

# Myth #2: Anxiety Isn't Really An Illness

While some form of anxiety is healthy, but anxiety disorder is not. It can cause impairment and thus is an illness and you need to get treated.

# Myth #3: Having Anxiety Is Very Uncommon

According to studies, one in five people on earth suffer from anxiety disorder. So, there is nothing to be ashamed of.

# Myth #4: An Anxiety Attack Can Lead To A Heart Attack

Panic attacks are frightening as they come with shortening of breath, chest pain and rapid beating of heart. It is common to think that a heart attack might follow or you are about to collapse. But these are all psychological responses and not physical ones. It is unlikely you do suffer from heart attack.

## Myth #5: All You Need To Treat Anxiety Is A Tranquilizer

Off the shelf pills can lessen or hide your symptoms only for a little time. A complete analysis and medication is advised for permanent relief.

Knowing the difference between what is real and what is a myth can help you on the path of overcoming your anxiety. While this journey will be long and hard, in the end it is completely worth it.

# Chapter Two: The Signs and Symptoms of An Anxiety Condition and The Various Types

Since all of us get anxious now and then, how do you decide if you have crossed the line from being anxious sometimes to being anxious all the time? Often the line is blurred. If you notice any of the below symptoms or signs frequently, then it is time to call your doctor:

## Sleeplessness

How is your sleep pattern? Do you toss and turn till its wee hours? Do you snore while sleeping or do you experience muscle weakness the next day morning? A disturbed sleep pattern along with respiratory problems is an indication of anxiety. Talk to your doctor about this.

One of the most frequent times that anxiety sufferers experience attacks is just before they fall asleep. This is the time of day when you have your thoughts to yourself and it is common for sufferers to lie awake for hours worrying.

More often than not, those with an anxiety disorder have difficulty sleeping. It is not unusual for people to have difficulty sleeping before an important event as they lie awake worrying about what may or may not occur. This is perfectly normal on the odd occasion , however, if you find yourself chronically lying awake, or if you find yourself waking up in the middle of the night because of your own worries, then something needs to be done.

# Stressed Out

Do you feel anxious about work, home and even outside during social gatherings? Do you feel worried why a person has not yet responded to your Facebook request even after a week? If you are constantly feeling stressed about every situation, it could be anxiety taking a toll on your life.

It can be difficult to determine if a person is worrying "too much" or are just simple stressed out. You can say that you are worrying excessively if it feels like your worries are getting in the way of your daily life. If your anxiety has already made you dysfunctional, then perhaps it is time for you to take a look at your situation seriously. If you worry too much for no real reason, then you may have an anxiety disorder.

# Increased Muscle Tension

Anxiety can manifest itself in physical ways. When you feel tension in your muscles because of stress, then your body is telling you that it is under too much pressure. One good way to handle muscle tension is through exercise, however those with an anxiety disorder may still experience a lot of muscle tension even if they exercise.

# Feeling Self-Conscious

In a sense, those with an anxiety disorder are people pleasers. They want to make sure that they look right and that they say the right things all the time. They are conscious of all their actions because they want to make sure that they won't do anything that will cause trouble. People with an anxiety disorder tend to feel like all eyes are on them. They are worried that people judge them for the things they do.

## Painful Headaches

Headaches are common. But, if you get them frequently along with weakness, dizziness and loss of sensation, then check with your doctor if anxiety is the reason.

## The Development of Phobias

If you have extreme reactions to some places, things, animals or birds, it is a form of anxiety disorder. A phobia that cannot be handled becomes an anxiety disorder. You don't know the reason yourself and you cannot control your reactions too. It is a phobia that is taking over your life.

## Feeling Shaky

Did you ever feel like things are shaking around you? Your vision is blurred and trees and cars are shaking. You have felt sometimes as though your legs, hands, fingers or entire body is shaking. This could be vertigo or major anxiety issue, consult your doctor and get it clarified.

## Indigestion

If you notice sudden stomach aches, weakness in underbelly frequently, then take it as a major symptom of anxiety disorder. If vomiting, nausea, diarrhea or constipation follows your stomach ailment, speak to your doctor to eliminate any other medical conditions.

Generally, the first common symptom is an irregular bowel movement.

# Types of Anxiety Disorders

Each experiences a different form of anxiety. Some have it as a general disorder , others have specific kinds. Some are due to social situations; a few are because of personal ideologies, and many have irrational fears. Here are serious seven types of it:

## 1. GAD or General Anxiety Disorder

This is a common form of worry over little things. Unprovoked reaction or over reaction to simple situation is GAD. For instance, getting paranoid over losing your wallet or over thinking and panicking about a discussion with your colleague are a few examples. It is a persistent situation where you just cannot stop worrying. Constant fatigue, restlessness, irritation or edginess is collective symptom of general anxiety disorder.

## 2. Social Phobia Disorder

It is very likely that you get butterflies in your stomach when you have to speak on public platforms. However, if you find it very difficult to socialize in public, there are chances you are suffering from a social phobia. You feel extremely shy in public or you are constantly worrying if you would say or do something stupid or embarrassing.

Do you live in the constant fear of being judged, remarked, observed or avoided upon? A familiar characteristic of social phobia is avoidance. You tend to avoid get together, parties in your defense to avoid any unpleasant situation.

## 3. Agoraphobia Disorder

Fear of unknown places or open spaces is termed as agoraphobia. This is prominent among adults. Generally accompanied with panic disorders. A person feels that he or she might end up getting a panic attack in an unknown place with unfamiliar people, putting themselves in an embarrassing and helpless situation. It is often noticed that a person with agoraphobia is scared to travel around. Thus, getting home bound, staying indoors, cutting out social contacts and complicating the situation further.

## 4. PTSD or Post-Traumatic Stress Disorder

(PTSD): Life is unpredictable, there are chances you have had some horrible physical or emotional traumas that have left a distressing mark on you. A loved ones death or a horrifying accident is an example. It is possible that just being witness to a situation can cause PTSD. Some of the symptoms include reliving the trauma, responding to a similar situation frantically or always being apprehensive that it can occur again. You might feel detached or disinterested, far worse you might become emotionally numb if not attended to.

# 5. OCD or Obsessive Compulsive Disorder

Obsessions are thought based while compulsions are supplementing actions towards an obsession. Obsessive thought is either fearful or negative. And, compulsions are doing an activity in a right way and you cannot stop yourself from not doing it, however hard you try. For example, you find it necessary to arrange your files in a specific order and till you don't have it your way, you are unable to focus or do anything else. Sometimes OCD's are very serious and can appear to disrupt yours as well as others around you. An activity becomes your habit, then gradually a ritual.

## 6. Panic Disorder

Panic disorder is not about panicking. It is about extreme worry that can affect your physical and mental wellbeing. Panic attacks are intense sensations across your body. There are also mental sensations that last about 10-15 minutes during a panic attack. You might feel helpless, hopeless; you might feel like you are doomed. However, the physical symptoms are more loud and clear. Sometimes the fear of a panic attack itself can get you one.

## 7. Specific Phobia Disorder

Like mentioned earlier, phobias are common. But when your life is affected frequently and goes into a troll, these phobias become anxiety disorders. Common phobias are being afraid of animals and insects such as snakes, spiders, cockroaches etc. However, when your reaction to such phobias is in a disastrous way, things are bound to worsen. For example, fear of water is not a good one. Then, you cannot take shower; you become hysteric if some waterfalls over you. Some people can live with their phobias, for example phobia of snakes, if you live in the city and do not come across them, then it doesn't even matter much.

There is nothing to be afraid of; you are not fighting it alone. If you have identified what kind of anxiety are you suffering from, then you are in the right direction. You can now help yourself, treat yourself and regain control over your life. There are several medications, supplements and therapies available. However, even before getting medical help, you can help yourself with some natural remedies, exercises, meditation and lifestyle changes.

# Chapter Three: Making The Transition To Regular Activities To Cure Your Anxiety

Anxiety cannot really be cured unless the core of the cause that produces it is dealt with. Any herbal approach will alleviate the symptoms but not the disease itself. If those symptoms are not severe to the point that professional opinion and care is essential, and you are otherwise quite capable of carrying on with your everyday life, then soothing agents can be used for the symptoms before any medical intervention.

If you have never tried alternative and natural methods to curing your anxiety. There are a few small things that you can do to get started. In this chapter you will learn what small steps you can take to begin the transition into natural ways to cure your anxiety so that you do not feel overwhelmed with the entire process.

# Tips To Starting Of On A Natural Anxiety Cure

## Chamomile Tea

There are some compounds in Chamomile Tea like matricaria recutita bind to the same brain receptors as tranquilizers. Chamomile can also be taken as a supplement standardized to contain 1.2% apigenin along with dried chamomile flowers. There is ample documentation of patients suffering from generalized anxiety disorder that took supplements for a period of 8 weeks and had a significant decrease in their symptoms.

## Green Tea

The next available herbal remedy is green tea. It contains an amino acid call L-theanine which is a substance that reduces a growing heart beat and blood pressure and a few human studies have shown that it reduces anxiety too. A dosage of 200 milligrams of this acid induces serenity and allows the subject to be more focused. To receive this dosage a minimum of 5 cups of green tea per day is required.

## Valerian

Valerian is a sleep aid for insomnia. It smells badly, therefore, most people consume it in the form of capsule or tincture, rather than tea. If you want to try it, please do so in the evening before going to bed, and not before going to work.

## A Touch of Lavender Here and There

The scent of lavender constitutes an anti-inflammatory for the emotions. One of the relevant studies showed that patients were less worried if the waiting room was perfumed with lavender. During another exam had less apprehension, although some students claimed it created ambiguity during the test. According to a third study, a lavender pill of a specific formulation was shown to reduce symptoms in people with Generalized Anxiety Disorder as effectively as lorazepam, which is an anti-anxiety medicine in the same category as Valium.

# Meditation

Meditation is a practice wherein a person induces an alternate level consciousness or trains his mind to practice stillness. There are a variety of techniques for promoting relaxation, establishing stillness, and building internal energy. When you meditate, you relax your mind and body. Meditation should be done in a quiet and peaceful place in order to attain peace of mind. You can do meditation alone or in a group.

Meditation can offer profound rest to your physiological self by activating a parasympathetic response in the nervous system, also known as the relaxation response. Essentially, rest is a natural way of getting rid of anxiety and stress. Your body is designed to eliminate stress when you sleep. Today, there are a lot of stressors around.

You can get stressed out from your daily activities, the people around you, and the situations that you are in. If you want to have a healthier mind and body, meditation may be the relief you have been looking for.

# Chapter Four: The Health Benefits of Using Natural Therapy Vs. Prescription Drug Use

Study after study has clearly shown that cardiovascular exercise and/ or weight training works just as well as antidepressant medication, but with one key advantage - Those subjects who treat their anxiety and depression with exercise tend to stay well, whereas those who treat their depression with medication have a significantly higher relapse rate.

And this is not just fringe research. This is mainstream research by reputable universities and scientific organizations , reported in renowned scientific journals. Whether you refer to the Mayo Clinic or the Black Dog Institute, all will recommend exercise therapy as a first-line tool to treat depression and anxiety.

So, if they evidence is so clear and there have been many studies conducted on the matter, why aren't doctors and specialists recommending this as the first form of treatment to treat a variety of anxiety disorders? There are many reasons:

## 1. Just Out of Habit

It is often hard for many doctors to change their minds on particular courses of treatment. The truth of the matter is that they like to stick to what they know works. This is especially true for many serious conditions such as anxiety, cancer and even heart disease.

While many doctors are keenly aware that those who suffer from severe anxiety and depression are more prone to dying from suicide, they will still stick to the course of treatment that they have seen work especially in those that have been able to avoid committing suicide.

## 2. Liability

If a doctor is open to any other course of treatment that deviates from their standard practice, they are at risk to legal liability. However, if a doctor were to stick to an acceptable practice, there is little to no risk of being sued. To be on the safe side, doctors would rather saves themselves then put themselves at risk for being sued in the future.

## Medications Work More Quickly

Doctors are convinced that prescription medication is more likely to work faster and more effectively then natural cures for anxiety and depression. This is not necessarily true as most antidepressants and relaxers usually will not start working on the patient until around the 4th week mark. To make matters worse most antidepressant treatments tend to make the condition worse before they can help effectively treat the condition.

It's clear that anxiety issues need to be treated. No one should have to cope with these severe symptoms on a daily basis. People who experience regular anxiety problems need to take steps to reduce the stress and anxiety in their lives.

Many people with anxiety simply turn to taking medication. It's true that medication can effectively treat anxiety. However, it comes at a price. Anxiety medication can cause severe side effects, including mania and hallucination. While these effects are rare, other troublesome effects, like confusion and nausea, are much more common.

Remember, anxiety medication can actually worsen symptoms of anxiety. Many people experience increased nervousness after taking medication. If an anxiety disorder is already serious, this can be incredibly dangerous. More anxiety is the last thing any anxiety sufferer needs in their lives.

Anyone considering medication should ask himself or herself whether or not this is truly the best way to treat their anxiety problem. They should know that the medication may not work, and that they'll have to deal with unpleasant side effects in exchange for relief. For many, the side effects simply aren't worth the benefits.

# The Benefits of Natural Cures For Anxiety

Many natural anxiety treatments have been researched extensively, and the results have been quite positive. In fact, many herbal ingredients are used in prescription anxiety medications. No one needs to take harsh drugs in order to treat their anxiety. They can take beneficial herbs on their own.

As researchers have continued to study natural treatment methods, their opinions have become more and more favorable. In fact, there are a number of doctors who advocate for these treatments over the standard prescription treatments. They've looked at the research, and determined that natural treatment is the better option by far.

In this section we will go through the many benefits of using natural remedies to cure your anxiety so you can learn why natural remedies are better for you than prescription medications.

# 1. Much More Affordable

Natural anxiety treatments can be far more affordable than prescription alternatives. Even with insurance, anxiety medication can be quite costly. Add in the cost of a doctor's visit, and anyone who takes medication can count on spending a great deal of money on his or her treatment.

In contrast, there's little to no cost associated with natural treatments. Many natural remedies involve things that people already have in their kitchen . Other remedies don't require any products at all. They simply give people the tools they need to improve their lives.

## 2. A Natural and Fast Way To Relax

When someone is overwhelmed by anxiety or experiencing a panic attack, they need a way to calm down quickly. If a panic attack goes untreated for too long, it can cause issues that require medical attention. This is doubly true if the panic attack sufferer already has health problems like a heart condition or asthma.

Breathing exercises can help you to relax naturally and fast so you can nip your panic attacks in the butt before they get worse.

## 3. No Harmful Side Effects

When you take prescription medications there is always a risk of side effects. Whether it is vomiting, nausea, increased suicidal thoughts, increased mood swings, sleepiness and fatigue.

With natural medication and natural remedies, this is something that you do not need to worry about. There are little to no side effects when using natural remedies and they are more likely to leave you feeling much better than much worse in the long run.

# Chapter Five: How To Best Deal With Your Anxiety

Once you realize how much time and energy you waste by worrying too much, you will likely want to manage your anxiety in order to be more productive. You will be surprised by how much more you can achieve once you get rid of excessive worrying. You can manage your anxiety in simple ways. Minor changes in your lifestyle have a significant impact in managing your anxiety and in return will dramatically improve the quality of your life.

Here are some tips that I have personally used myself and will help you handle your panic attacks in a better way.

# Taking Care of Your Body

There is a strong relationship between mind, emotion and body. It will be easier to relax if you know that you are taking care of your body. Try to develop healthy eating and fitness eating habits. Exercise and a clean diet can do wonders for your anxiety.

Also, try to sleep well and on time. If you have a healthy routine, you will have more energy to actually face and handle the ups and downs of life. Make wise food choices, develop a good sleeping habit and exercise regularly. It sounds far too simple, but this too has been one of the biggest factors to my success in overcoming anxiety.

# Talk About Your Problems With Other People

It helps if you have a trusted friend or relative who is willing to listen to your worries. Trying to contain your feelings can be very challenging. It will just allow your panic to snowball. When a person is willing to listen to your problems and vulnerabilities, you will be a bit more at ease and will realize that firstly you are not alone, and secondly things aren't as bad as they seem.

Do not always expect that the other person will be able to comfort you completely. It is highly unlikely that the other person will be able to erase all your worries . However, talking about worries will prevent them from becoming bigger and bigger. It will prevent you from snapping at a random situation. Talking about your problems will prevent you from exploding and may assist you in maintaining perspective.

## Try Connecting With Nature

There is something about the harmony of nature which is incredibly calming and relaxing. Allow yourself to be comforted by the beauty of the universe. Find solace in parks or gardens. Choose a place which will make you feel safe and grounded. If you want, you can even ask a friend to accompany you as you enjoy nature's wonders. I personally love sitting on a bench in a park on a quiet Sunday morning and just watching the world go by. I may choose to read a book, or simply sit and contemplate life and my surroundings. This has an amazing calming effect on me and really allows me to ensure I see the world in all its beauty and splendor.

You can also engage in a hobby involving nature. Gardening or mountain climbing is a good way to improve your relationship with the wonders around you. You'll be surprised by what a little sunshine can do in your life. You will feel lighter, better and maybe even happier.

## Try To Be Grateful

To be honest, there are a million and one ways that things can go wrong in every moment. Your situation could be much worse than it actually is. Try to focus on the good things that are happening in your life . Look for things that you can be grateful for. Do you have a roof above your head? Are there people in your life that make you smile? If you focus on the good things that happen in your life, it is very likely that you will feel less anxious about what the future holds.

I like to call these moments my "magic moments" as I reflect on all the good things I have going for me in my life. It immediately helps calm me and once again acts as a great leveler to my worries and anxiety.

## Learn To Delegate Your Tasks Effectively

Don't try to do everything, especially if you are part of a team. Having too many tasks at hand will just give you more reason to worry. You will find yourself overwhelmed if you don't know how to trust that other people can complete their tasks. Don't assume all responsibility. There is a good chance that there are other people who can and will help make a task easier for you.

# Try To Learn To Calm Yourself Down

People sometimes become slaves of their own feelings . If you are anxious, you need to learn how to find your own peace of mind. Find your own "calm" place. This means knowing how to take charge when it seems like your emotions are taking over. There are many various ways to calm yourself down.

# Don't Try To Micro Manage Everything

Those who have anxiety disorders often focus on the tiniest details. Sometimes, they worry about things which are not really important. Stop trying to focus on every single detail of every single task. Trying to focus on everything will just tire you out. L earn how to determine and focus on the important parts of the equation, which truly deserve your attention.

Do not make a big fuss out of things that don't really matter.

## Learn To Keep Yourself Busy

If you are an anxiety sufferer, it is highly likely that you will spend your free time worrying about unimportant things. Try to minimize your idle time so that you won't spend too much time worrying about things that don't really matter. It is best to try and get a hobby to fill up your free time. Find something that interests you. It is a good idea to get into art or sports. Aside from keeping you busy, it will also help you use up your energy so you won't have excess energy to worry about silly things that don't matter.

# Try To Manage Your Sleeping Habits A Bit Better

Sleep is very important. It allows your brain to rest and re-charge. However, it can be difficult to sleep of you have a lot of worries on your mind. Exert conscious effort to follow a sleeping routine. Prepare your body for sleeping time. Exert effort to have a beautiful rest every night so that your brain will feel more relaxed in the morning.

## Attack Uncertainty Head On

One of the best things I've learnt in the last few years is that the best way to deal with uncertainty is to attack it. Are you anxious about your job? Attack it! Go at it with such gusto that you excel at it and achieve fantastic results. Are you worried about losing weight or training for a running race? Attack it! Train as if you have to run a marathon, and whatever you are trying to achieve will seem easy in comparison.

Uncertainty can be a huge contributor to anxiety, and the best way to deal with it is to attack it. This has been one of the greatest things I've focused on and it has made a huge difference to my anxiety levels.

# Chapter Six: Natural Strategies To Use To Reduce Your Anxiety

Anyone considering medication should ask himself or herself whether or not this is truly the best way to treat their anxiety problem. They should know that the medication may not work, and that they'll have to deal with unpleasant side effects in exchange for relief. For many, the side effects simply aren't worth the benefits.

Thankfully, there's a far better way to treat anxiety. People have successfully been using natural anxiety remedies for thousands of years. There are a number of natural cures that can help people deal with their anxiety symptoms, while sparing them from the harsh side effects of medication.

In this chapter you will learn a variety of different natural strategies to use to help control and cure your anxiety.

## Treating Your Anxiety With Tea

Tea has the power to relieve anxiety on a number of levels. The very act of drinking tea is relaxing , particularly when that tea is hot. It also requires people to take a few minutes to sit and relax, something that anxiety sufferers need badly.

It creates a positive routine, which is relaxing in and of itself. Studies have shown that following calming routines can play a role in reducing anxiety symptoms. In addition, tea provides the body with the hydration it needs to fight back against anxiety symptoms.

However, the real benefit of teas comes from the herbs they contain. Many herbs found in tea can provide long-term anxiety relief. Drinking tea made from fresh herbs can have a particularly beneficial effect, but even packaged tea can be quite helpful.

One type of tea that it particularly good at easing tension is valerian root. This herb is a natural sedative, and can help the body to process emotions more effectively. It works particularly well for people who are unable to get enough sleep because of their anxiety. However, it should be noted that this tea could cause some people to feel lethargic.

Research has shown that blue vervain can calm the nervous system, and can effectively treat a number of nervous conditions. It can also help people get a more restful night's sleep. However, even though this tea works very well, experts recommend against drinking it regularly. It's better for occasional relief.

You can also use Chamomile Tea. Chamomile tea is famous for its ability to aid in relaxation. It soothes a number of anxiety symptoms, and can also calm a nervous stomach. People who have experienced a reduction in appetite because of their stress should give chamomile a try. It may provide them with anxiety relief while restoring their appetite.

One of the advantages of chamomile is that children can safely consume this tea. Many children suffer from anxiety as well, and this natural relief method can help them cope with their symptoms. However, when it comes to people under the age of twelve, it's recommended that chamomile not be taken for an extended period of time.

Another type of tea that you can also use is Lemon Balm Tea. Lemon balm tea works to soothe the nervous system, reducing feelings of anxiety and stress. It also has the power to relieve headaches, which are commonly experienced by people with anxiety disorders. Those who don't enjoy hot tea can experience the soothing properties of lemon balm tea by drinking it iced.

Green tea is also another type of tea that you can use to help treat your anxiety as long as you drink decaffeinated tea. Most green tea contains caffeine, which means that many anxiety sufferers often avoid it. However, it also contains a substance called theanine, which helps to promote alpha waves in the brain. This can provide a significant amount of relaxation. Decaffeinated green tea allows people to reap the benefits of theanine while avoiding the negative side effects of caffeine.

Tea can ease the symptoms of anxiety on a number of levels. It's a good idea for anxiety sufferers to experiment with different teas, as this allows them to see which types provide them with the most relief. Some teas are more effective when taken daily, while others should only be taken on occasion.

Tea is healthy, calming, and can benefit the mind and body in a number of ways. It's more than a beverage, it's a potent way to treat health problems and reduce stress. Tea should be a part of any anxiety sufferer's life.

## Treating Your Anxiety With Whole Foods

When treating anxiety, nothing is as safe as simple as consuming the right foods. A number of foods have natural calming properties, and a number of nutrients can help the body fight back against anxiety. With a diet rich in whole foods, managing anxiety can become far easier.

Foods rich in tryptophan increase the amount of serotonin produced by the body, which can help people keep people calm and happy. In addition, researchers believe that a lack of serotonin can cause anxiety. Studies have found that people with anxiety disorders have far less serotonin in their blood.

A wide range of foods contain tryptophan. Bananas, nuts, and soy are all good sources of tryptophan , as are lean proteins like turkey and chicken. Tryptophan can also be found in most dairy products.

Healthy carbohydrates can also help to increase serotonin production. One of the best sources of good carbohydrates is whole grains. Whole wheat bread , brown rice, and oats can all provide an instant mood lift and a gradual reduction in anxiety symptoms.

There are certain chemicals and nutrients that you will want to make sure that you consume on a daily basis to help alleviate the symptoms of anxiety. These nutrients include Dopamine and Norepinephrine. These substance can help reduce the symptoms of anxiety by improving the function of nerve cells. This can have a calming effect, but it can also be quite energizing. Foods that contain these substances are a great way to reduce anxiety symptoms without inducing lethargy.

So, what foods can you consume that contain these substances? Protein. Protein-rich foods are the best source of norepinephrine and dopamine. Greek yogurt is a particularly good food to consume, as are nuts, beans, and lentils . Fish, meat, and eggs are also full of protein, and can have a positive effect.

# Treating Anxiety With Acupuncture

For years, Western people approached acupuncture with skepticism. They didn't understand how sticking needles into the body could relieve anxiety symptoms. In fact, many people thought that the practice of acupuncture should cause people to experience more anxiety.

It's easy to see why people have such a hard time wrapping their heads around the concept of acupuncture. Acupuncture is based on the ancient Chinese principle of qi. Proponents of acupuncture believe that correctly balancing qi in the body can cure a number of ailments. While the concept of qi hasn't been sufficiently studied, recent research has helped prove that acupuncture really can provide anxiety relief. More importantly, it has been discovered why it's so effective.

When the body is stressed, a number of hormones are secreted. These hormones affect the pituitary gland and the adrenal gland, and cause many of the symptoms most commonly associated with anxiety. These hormones can also trigger the " fight or flight" response, which can lead to panic attacks.

However, acupuncture is able to block these stress-induced hormone elevations. It can change the way blood circulates in the body, and can improve overall nerve function. Study after study has demonstrated that acupuncture really works.

What's interesting about acupuncture is that it provides both instantaneous and long-term relief. When someone sees an acupuncturist, they should feel immediate relief, even if they are uncomfortable around needles. However, those feelings of diminished anxiety should continue for several more weeks.

Although acupuncture was once considered to be alternative medicine, its increased legitimacy has led to acupuncture treatments being covered by a number of insurance companies. This gives many people the opportunity to take advantage of one of the most effective anxiety treatments available.

It is important to note that acupuncture simply isn't for everyone. Some people may not be comfortable with the unusual nature of the treatment. Others may not have a reliable acupuncturist in their area. However, those who are willing to give acupuncture a try can experience a number of powerful benefits.

# Chapter Seven: Exercise and Anxiety and How One Can Help Alleviate The Other

People who suffer from anxiety may not be interested in exercise. When someone is overwhelmed by the stress of everyday life, working out seems less than appealing. However, research shows that exercise plays an important role in reducing anxiety symptoms.

While exercise has been clinically proven to reduce anxiety and improve mood, it can also treat a number of other health problems. Health issues can be a major anxiety trigger, and easing the symptoms of those ailments can reduce anxiety symptoms further.

In addition, exercising can help people relax. When a person exercises, their body releases hormones that produce a calming effect. Exercise also increases body temperature, which can be very relaxing. Working up a sweat is tiring, but it's a great way to calm down.

When some people hear the work "exercise," they picture a gym full of people lifting weights. However, there are many fitness activities that can provide the exercise someone with anxiety needs. Even everyday activities like gardening or washing a car can elevate the mood.

Many people think they don't have time for exercise, but exercise doesn't have to take hours. Instead, people can find little ways to increase physical activity throughout the day. They might stretch at their desk at work, or take a quick walk during their lunch break.

Studies suggest that 30 minutes of exercise a day, three days a week can dramatically reduce anxiety symptoms. However, those same studies show that even small amounts of activity can have a positive effect. If someone doesn't have time for lengthy workouts, they should still find ways to get the exercise their body needs.

While increase physical activity provides a number of health benefits, they aren't lasting. In order for exercise to improve anxiety, it must be done on a consistent basis. That makes it all the more important for people to find exercise routines they can stick with, and physical activities that they enjoy.

For many people who suffer from anxiety, beginning an exercise routine is the hardest part. Once they get started, however, they find these periods of physical activity to be one of the most enjoyable parts of the day. Sticking with an exercise routine can be very easy if that routine is planned out well.

Anyone beginning an exercise routine should think about the physical activities they enjoy most. Do they enjoy playing with their children? Riding a bicycle? Gardening in their backyard? When it comes to reducing anxiety symptoms, any activity that gets the body moving counts as exercise.

No one should feel as though they have to decide on a workout plan and stick to it forever. Sampling a variety of different activities can help keep motivation levels high. Different kinds of exercises have different benefits, and switching between them gives people the chance to experience them all.

## Low Impact Exercises

Swimming is a low-impact way to burn calories and get the body into shape. People who try lots of activities will be able to discover what suits them best . They may also find that they prefer to alternate the types of exercise they do.

While low-impact exercises are easier for people who are new to exercise, more intense exercise can also have a very positive effect. For example, running or long-distance jogging provides something that's called a "runner's high". This is a wave of positive emotion that hits a person after a long run. People who are up for the challenge should definitely take advantage of intense workouts.

## Set Reasonable Goals and Take Your Time With Exercise

It is important to set reasonable goals. When people set plans they can't stick to, they feel discouraged. People should think realistically about what they have time for and what they'll be able to do. Their plan should be tailored to their own unique needs and abilities.

When adjusting to a workout routine, there will be setbacks and obstacles. Sometimes people will get too busy for exercise, or sometimes they will simply forget. No one should take these missteps as a sign they've failed or should give up. Instead, they should try again the following day.

I highly recommend using a workout journal when it comes to getting into the routine of working out. When you can see all their successes in print, missing a workout feels less like a failure. In addition, writing things down will allow you to track how much your workouts have improved your anxiety symptoms. Some people may find that certain types of exercises give them better results.

Exercise should never feel like a chore. If workouts are treated like an obligation, people may feel like a failure when they don't have time for them. Instead, exercise should be treated as a tool. It's one of many things that people with anxiety can do if they want to get better.

Remember, exercise isn't a cure-all, but it can be a tremendous help. People will get more out of workouts if they also eat well, take supplements , and focus on treating their anxiety in other ways. Physical activity is an excellent way to ease the symptoms of anxiety, but it shouldn't be the only thing a person does to get anxiety relief.

# Relaxation Exercises To Use To Help Reduce Your Anxiety

Anyone who suffers from anxiety should familiarize themselves with relaxation exercises. Relaxation exercises trigger the body's relaxation response, and work to calm the nervous system. These exercises help make the body relaxed, calm, and focused.

Experts suggest that anxiety sufferers should set aside 10 to 20 minutes a day for relaxation exercises. As people get more comfortable with these exercises , they may find that they can accomplish more in a shorter time period. The most important thing is that the exercises are done consistently.

In this section you will learn the best exercise techniques to use and how they will help to reduce your anxiety symptoms.

# Breathing Meditation

One of the most common relaxation exercises is breathing meditation. This technique focuses on taking deep, cleansing breaths. Breathing meditation is easy to learn, and can be practiced no matter where a person is. This makes it a powerful tool that anxiety sufferers can use to cope with stressful situations.

Many people combine breathing meditation with other relaxation techniques, such as music, or aromatherapy. Using lavender while focusing on breathing can be particularly helpful.

Breathing meditation involves breathing from the abdomen, filling the lungs with fresh air. This causes the body to inhale more oxygen, which reduces anxiety. Typically, people take shallow breaths from their chest, which can lead to feelings of tension. As people practice this type of breathing, they'll begin taking deeper breaths even when they're not meditating.

People can begin these exercises by lying on their back. From there, they should place one hand on their chest, and one on their stomach. They should then exhale through their mouth; pushing out all the air they can while contracting their abdominal muscles. The hand on the stomach should move slightly, but the other should remain still.

After that, the individual should continue to breathe in through their nose and out through their mouth. They should inhale in a way that causes their lower abdomen to rise and fall. While exhaling, they should count downwards slowly.

# Progressive Muscle Relaxation

A quick version of this can be done in the case of a panic attack, but a more in-depth version can provide someone with a deep awareness of what tension feels like throughout the body. This can make it easier for them to relax themselves when they're feeling anxious.

In order for this exercise to be at its most effective, people should wear loose clothing and remove their shoes. Pajamas are ideal. Additionally, it should be done in a quiet, open place.

The first step of progressive muscle relaxation is to take slow, deep breaths. Once a person is relaxed, they should tense the muscles in their right foot, squeezing it, and holding it for ten seconds. After that, they should relax the foot, focusing on the feeling of tension fading away.

From there, they should move to the left foot, and then on to the right calf. They should move slowly throughout their body until every muscle has been relaxed. While this exercise can take a long time at first, it can be done very quickly once a person is familiar with the process.

## Visual Meditation

Also known as guided imagery, this technique involves imagining a scene that will allow a person to let go of their tension . In order for this relaxation exercise to be effective, it should be done in a quiet room, free from disturbances.

Before beginning , the person using the technique should select a scene that makes them feel calm. This could be a white-sand beach, a beautiful forest, or a field full of flowers. Some people find that this technique is more effective when accompanied by sounds that match their chosen setting.

This technique should be done with eyes closed. From there, the next step is to picture the chosen place, imagining it in as much detail as possible . From there, a scenario is imagined that will make them feel particularly relaxed.

If their calm place is a beach , they might imagine walking around the sand looking for seashells and dipping their toes in the water. If they've chosen a park, they might imagine sitting on a bench and feeding the birds. Sensory details should be incorporated as much as possible.

## Tai Chi and Yoga

Both yoga and tai chi are also effective relaxation exercises. In fact, yoga can improve the body's relaxation response in day-to-day life. These exercises are slow paced and not at all strenuous, making them a good fit for people of all ages.

Those who are unfamiliar with yoga and tai chi may want to begin by taking a class. Some moves are hard to imitate without seeing them in motion. Video footage is also an option.

From deep breathing to full-body stretches, relaxation exercises have the potential to provide relation on both a long-term and short-term basis. Once these techniques become a regular part of a person's life, they'll find that they feel far calmer, and experience far less anxiety.

Relaxation exercises can provide people with a great deal of control over their anxiety symptoms. When regularly practiced, these techniques can help people to experience fewer symptoms and far fewer panic attacks. They're something anxiety sufferers should familiarize themselves with.

# Chapter Eight: How To Help Someone Suffering From Anxiety

Living with someone who has anxiety problems can be quite a challenge. You need to be more sensitive about their condition because they are already having a lot of difficulties. You can't expect them to calm down easily. You need to know how to act around them so that you can show your support and understanding regarding their situation.

Do you live with someone who has anxiety or panic disorder? Here are the things that you should keep in mind.

# Do Not Offer Alcohol As A Way To Deal With Their Anxiety

Perhaps alcohol can provide short-term help, however in the long run, it might be a gateway for addiction. Alcohol can be relaxing at the beginning, but it can actually reinforce anxiety and panic.

Furthermore, alcohol can increase the actual problems significantly. Drinking too much can lead to certain unwanted actions and situations. It is not a good idea to make an anxious person think that alcohol can help them solve his or her problems.

## Try Not To Trivialize The Problem

It can be tempting to point out how small the problems are. This is especially true if you are suffering problems of your own. No matter how stressed out you are, resist the urge to talk about your own problems.

To a certain extent, talking about problems and anxieties can be stressful. It can even destroy relationships and camaraderie if you talk about problems too much . If you are suffering problem of your own, it would be best to just distance yourself from the anxious person so that you won't use your anxieties as a basis for bonding together.

## Set Boundaries

It is only natural that you would want to help in any way you can. However, helping your partner too much might actually be more harmful. Do not feed your loved one's anxiety by being too available. Try to distance yourself sometimes. It will teach your loved one to be independent step by step while still allowing you to remain sensitive and helpful when they need it most.

## Don't Expect The Person To Calm Down Easily

When you tell an anxious person to calm down, although it is likely that you have very good intensions , it does not mean that you will be able to help. Think about it, if a person was able to calm themselves down, then he or she probably would done so already. It is important to keep in mind that these people are not in complete control of their feelings. Telling them to calm down may just make them panic even more.

In my experience, it is best to allow them to be anxious for a while and let them ride it out. Listen to what they have to say until they have calmed down. You can even offer to do something distracting to keep their mind off their worries.

## Don't Try "Tough Love"

In certain types of personalities, tough love might indeed work, however for those with an anxiety disorder; it is likely that this method will not be effective . Tough love will more often than not just make them feel weak, and generally incapable of achieving anything. Try to be more sensitive in choosing words that will encourage them.

## Encourage Them To Seek Treatment

As soon as you realize that you are not in the position to make things better, it is best to seek professional help. Anxiety, especially in milder cases, is highly treatable. You just have to start with convincing your loved one to seek professional help . Medication is even available to help your anxious loved one deal with the problem. However always seek the advice of professionals before starting any medical routine.

## Help Them To See The Good In Life

You need to make your partner understand that there is a better life out there. In order to enjoy more, he or she just has to let go of all worries. You have to make your loved one WANT to change without being forceful. Only by truly desiring a better life will a person start to improve his or her condition for the better.

Be supportive and loving, but show your partner how much better life can be once he or she panics less. This can be a little tricky but you have to find the balance between sending the message and being considerate.

# Conclusion

When people start experiencing anxiety symptoms, many friends and family members will suggest that they start taking prescription medication. However, that's not at all necessary, and can even be detrimental. Many anxiety issues can be treated very effectively with natural remedies.

Medication can cause harmful side effects, and can be costly. Natural remedies are a far safer option. While the right medication does have the ability to reduce anxiety symptoms, the right natural remedy can both reduce anxiety symptoms and improve health.

There are a number of natural treatment options that are both simple and effective.

Herbal teas can have extremely positive effects. Many people treat their anxiety with supplements, while others still treat it using food. However , in most cases, a combination of these will work best.

Some people opt to treat anxiety with alternative methods, such as homeopathy or acupuncture. Recent research has shown that both of these treatment options can be quite effective, and both these options are also quite safe . They're a good choice for anyone who is open to the possibility.

Exercise can also be an excellent way to reduce anxiety symptoms. When people are experiencing severe anxiety symptoms, they may not feel as though they can handle regular workouts. However, even a small increase in physical activity can have a positive effect. People who find little ways to exercise will see significant improvement in their symptoms.

While physical exercise is extremely beneficial, mental relaxation exercises can also help a great deal. These exercises may include deep breathing, guided imagery, or muscle relaxation techniques. They can provide people with a better understanding of their body and how it responds to anxiety.

Some exercises , such as yoga and tai chi, combine physical exercise with mental exercise, providing the best of both worlds. These exercises can help most anxiety sufferers tremendously. Because these exercises are low impact, it's easy for most people to do them, even if they're elderly or have other health problems.

In addition to long-term remedies, it's important that people also have a way to get fast anxiety relief. There are a number of quick and easy natural fixes that can help someone calm down if they feel as though they might be on the verge of a panic attack.

More importantly, people who experience anxiety should try to get to the root of their issues . Natural remedies should be seen treatment, not a cure. People should still work to find out what causes their anxiety, and take the steps necessary to reduce the amount of stress in their lives.

All the natural remedies suggested in this book can be helpful, but that doesn't mean everyone should use them. Women who are pregnant, or people with chronic health conditions, may want to talk to their doctor before trying a remedy. Most natural remedies are very safe, but that doesn't mean that caution isn't important.

The truth of the matter is that medication isn't what's going to help a person with anxiety.

What will help them is taking care of their body and working to resolve the stress in their lives. When people take better care of themselves, they'll experience less stress, and less anxiety in turn.

These natural remedies are incredibly simple, and can help anxiety sufferers in a variety of ways. Any anxiety sufferer can take advantage of this knowledge and take steps to improve their life.

Living with anxiety is hard, but it doesn't have to be that way. When people work to address their symptoms in a natural way, they can live a happier, more fulfilling life.

# About Us:

The Thought Flame is committed to add value to its customers through various books, online courses and other resources. You can learn more about us and our books at www.thethoughtflame.com.

Don't forget to check out our amazing **online video courses** at www.thethoughtflame.com/courses/ to take your knowledge to another level.

To check out our **extraordinary collection of diet/cookbooks**, visit http://www.thethoughtflame.com/category/non-fictional/cookbooks/ .

As a part of our valued relationship with our customers, we keep providing you free promotional books, courses and other stuff on subscribing with us on our site. We have a strict anti-spam policy and assure you no spam mails will be sent to your mailbox.

To subscribe with us, visit www.thethoughtflame.com.

Like our work and would like to say thanks?

Buy us a cup of coffee at www.thethoughtflame.com/coffee/

# **Author:**

Amarpreet Singh is an avid learner and his passion for education has made him travel, work and study all across the world. He holds three masters degrees, including MBA, from top universities in Asia.

He is author of dozens of books, many of which are Amazon's bestseller, varying in various topics and categories. He also teaches many online courses having thousands of students across the world.

He has a keen interest in international affairs, economics, global poverty and politics, financial markets and entrepreneurship, and strives to be part of a community that shares the same passion.

He has worked as consultant with organizations like Airbus and The World Bank. He loves travelling and learning about new cultures, and has been fortunate to live/work/travel/study in countries like India, China, Korea, US, South Africa, Japan, Philippines, Singapore, Canada etc., and learn about the culture and lifestyle in each of them.

To check out more of his work, visit www.thethoughtflame.com

www.ingramcontent.com/pod-product-compliance
Lightning Source LLC
Chambersburg PA
CBHW050413290526
45786CB00003B/1246